Fallen Rook Publishing

The Art of Defence on Foot, 1798

Part of the Academy of Historical Arts Facsimile series.

Author:
Charles Roworth (1798)

Facsimile Creator:
Ben Kerr (2014)

Facsimile Editor:
Keith Farrell (2014)

1st Edition
14th October 2014
ISBN 978-0-9926735-2-9
Published by Fallen Rook Publishing

The Academy of Historical Arts and Fallen Rook Publishing are divisions
within Triquetra Services (Scotland), a charitable organisation registered
in Scotland: registration number SC042086.

Version and Copyright Information

Version: 1st Edition
Date: 14th October 2014
Copyright © Ben Kerr, 2014
ISBN 978-0-9926735-2-9

Publisher

This book has been published by Fallen Rook Publishing, a division of Triquetra Services (Scotland), which is a charity registered in Scotland with number SC042086; published in Glasgow, United Kingdom, in October 2014.

Foreword

It was a bright Monday morning in late June when, beginning my work for the day, I came across an image I recognised from Roworth's *The Art of Defence*. Following this link, I realised that there was a fantastic copy of the book available for sale. Upon discussing the matter with my colleague Keith, we decided that our organisation did not have the available funds to make such a purchase. This was a shame, yet when I mentioned the book to some friends, David Britten of the Glasgow Company of Duellists encouraged us to set up a crowdfunding campaign. I discussed the idea with Keith again, and we decided to try this method for raising funds to make the purchase. We attempted to raise £500 towards the purchase, with our organisation making up the shortfall.

Within five hours of launch, the community had rallied to the cause and had raised the £500 requested. And this was only the beginning! Over the next two weeks, an increased £2125 was raised from the donations of 89 very generous individuals from all over the world. By the end of the first week of the campaign, an original copy of Roworth's 1798 treatise was sitting in my hands, and we had also bought some original posters of Angelo's system from the same era.

For me, the campaign was only the first step of the journey. Over the following months, I worked tirelessly to photograph every page to create the facsimile. The creative process has been extremely demanding, and through undertaking the project, I have learned a great deal about photography and working with old documents.

I have done my best to preserve the pages as I found them. This means that some of the letters are a little smudged, and in some places the ink is not as clear as would be ideal. I would have loved to provide the images as special fold-out pages, but the parameters of printing made this impossible. With this being said, I promise that to the best of my ability I have recreated the original book, and I hope that by reading the facsimile you will find yourself just that little bit closer to the past and to Roworth himself.

Sincerely,

Ben Kerr MA MLitt
Senior Instructor
Academy of Historical Arts
Triquetra Services (Scotland)
Registered Charity (SC042086)

Acknowledgements

The creation of this facsimile could not have been done alone and I would like to thank the following people for their assistance.

Keith Farrell was instrumental during the campaign and in assisting with the purchases of the original pieces. During the facsimile creation he has been a constant source of strength and encouragement to see the project through to completion.

It is often said for every journey that the hardest part is the first step, in this case I must thank Dave Britten for giving us the nudge out the door and on with this journey.

The Historical Community spread the message of the campaign and many contributed either financially or by ensuring the message would reach others who would contribute.

Finally although we would like to thank all our contributors the following people made substantial financial contributions to the project:

Alex Grant	Michelle Chu
B Kendall Ward	Owen Brighurst
Ben Hutchison	Robbie McDicken
Jeremy Loose	Robert Stewart
Jonathan M Gordon	Ross Bailey
Kieren Smith	Scott Aldinger
Laura Hogg	Scott Nimmo
Maksim Solovjov	Shannon Walker
Mark McMorrow	Stewart Palmer

The Long 'S'

by Ben Kerr

Due to the period during which this book was printed, throughout the text we see the regular appearance of a character that is no longer present in the English language. This character is the long 's' which is printed as ' ſ '. Although to the modern reader the character appears similar to a lower case 'f', it is printed either entirely without the central bar, or with only the left bar. It is not pronounced as 'f' but rather just as a normal 's', and used very similarly. In almost all cases, it only appears at the beginning or in the middle of a word.

Following the differentiation between capital and lower case characters in the 8th century, it was no longer used as the terminal character of a word, except in Italy between 1465 and 1480. The form of the character comes from Roman cursive script. [1]

The decline in its use is attributed to William Caslon's unnamed modern font, designed for John Bell of the British Letter Foundry.[2] Caslon was such a famous typeface designer that a common phrase came into fashion regarding choice of typeface: "when in doubt, use Caslon".[3] In 1791, "the general abolition of long *s* began" when Bell published a large collection of plays in an anthology named *British Theatre*, using Caslon's new font.[4] 17 years later, the 1808 typeface industry catalogue *Printer's Grammar* by Caleb Stower states that:

> "The introduction of the round s, instead of the long, is an improvement in the art of printing equal, if not superior, to any which has taken place in recent years, and for which we are indebted to the ingenious Mr. Bell, who introduced them in his edition of the *British Classics* [published in the 1780s and 1790s]. They are now generally adopted, and the founders [typefounders] scarcely ever cast a long s to their fonts, unless particularly ordered. Indeed, they omit it altogether in their specimens.... They are placed in our list of sorts, not to recommend them, but because we may not be subject to blame from those of the old school, who are tenacious of deviating from custom, however antiquated, for giving a list which they might term imperfect."

The transition by British printers away from printing books with the long 's' occurred between the 1798 edition of Roworth's fencing treatise and the 1804 edition, in which all the long 's' characters were printed as the modern, or short, 's'.

1   Lyn Davies. *A is for Ox*. London: Folio Society, 2006.
2   Michael Suarez. *The Oxford Companion to the Book*. Oxford: Oxford University Press, 2010.
3   Johnson Ball. *William Caslon, 1693–1766: the ancestry, life and connections of England's foremost letter-engraver and type-founder*. Kineton: Roundwood Press, 1973.
4   P.W. Nash. "The Abandonment of the Long *s* in Britain in 1800." *Journal of the Printing Historical Society* 3, (2001): 3-19.

A Brief Biography of Charles Roworth

by Keith Farrell

Charles Roworth was most likely born in the 1770s.[1] His parents were William and Mary Roworth, who owned a haberdashery shop in Islington,[2] a borough in London. Rather than following in exactly the same footsteps as his parents, Charles worked as a printer throughout his adult life, although he did follow their example and owned his own printing shop.[3] Printing was his profession, for which he was renowned, and he printed several books and posters for publishers such as Thomas Egerton and individuals such as Henry Angelo. It was not just books and posters about military subjects that he printed, he had a broad remit – for example, he was engaged to print one of the three volumes of Jane Austen's *Pride and Prejudice* when it was first published in 1812,[4] along with some of her other work, including *Emma* in 1815.[5]

He was also a keen fencer. He was a friend of the Angelo family of riding and fencing masters, and practised at their school.[6] However, he was not a qualified master, merely an enthusiastic and well-read amateur. In some ways, he could be regarded as a historical fencer in his own right, having read earlier fencing treatises such as *The Use of the Broad Sword* by Thomas Page (1746).[7] He incorporated elements of Page's work into his own book on fencing, *The Art of Defence on Foot, with the Broad Sword and Sabre*, which he printed in 1798.

This book seems to bear many similarities to the system of fencing developed by Henry Angelo in 1795, which became the regulation method for the British Army in 1796.[8] A reader may gain a reasonable understanding of the state of British military use of the broadsword and sabre in the final decade of the 18th century by studying Roworth's treatise along with Angelo's *Hungarian and Highland Broadsword* (1798) and *The Guards and Lessons of the Highland Broadsword* (1799).[9] Roworth was the printer involved in both of these projects of Angelo, and although his own book was the first of these three publications to reach completion, we do not know the order in which the projects were initiated or commissioned.[10]

In 1796, in response to fears of a French invasion, Britain raised some part-time volunteer militia regiments to help defend the nation. One of these regiments was the Westminster Light Horse Volunteers, in which Roworth enrolled when it formed.[11] It was in this regiment that he met John Taylor, the broadsword master from whom he learned the "ten lessons" that are included in the second edition of his book. In 1806, after the Battle of Trafalgar in the previous year had ended any chance of a French invasion, these volunteer regiments were disbanded.

1796 was a big year for Roworth. As well as becoming a volunteer cavalryman, he and his wife Ann had their first son, Henry.[12] In 1803 they had a second son,

Charles William.[13] His two sons grew up to join him in the family printing business, becoming partners in 1832.[14]

Roworth's book was expanded and reprinted in 1804, and was popular enough to warrant an American edition in 1824. The work was also popular within Britain, and was considered a respectable enough authority on the science of arms that John Wilkes plagiarised seventy-five pages of Roworth's original text for inclusion in the *Encyclopaedia Londinensis*.[15] In 1807, Roworth brought a court case against Wilkes for piracy. Although the law was not on his side, the case was decided in his favour, and Roworth was awarded £100 in damages.[16] The presiding judge, Lord Ellenborough, stated that common law should be able to protect an author, even if the text did not bear the author's name.[17] This court case led to a development in copyright law in Britain, helping to shape modern copyright legislation.[18]

Roworth continued to print books after this case. He was no stranger to the courtroom, it seems, as he pressed charges of common larceny against Thomas Wilson in 1831 for stealing paper from his shop.[19]

However, we have little further information about the man and his activities. The publishing company that he ran in partnership with his sons changed name and location several times,[20] and he remained involved in the business until he died in 1869.[21] Three years later, in 1872, his sons Henry and Charles William dissolved the business.[22] In 1874, Henry also passed away, surviving his father by only five years.[23]

To the field of historical fencing, Roworth provided an immensely important addition of technical literature. He was not a qualified master of fencing, but he had many noteworthy insights, and provided a clear and valuable textual description of his system.

On behalf of Fallen Rook Publishing, we hope you enjoy and appreciate this facsimile.

1   In 1796 his son Henry was born, making it unlikely that Charles himself was born any later than 1778. Charles died in 1869, so it is unlikely that he would have been born much earlier than the 1770s. However, his parents did have a child in 1767, which may have been Charles or an older sibling; the latter is the more likely option, since Charles would have died aged 102 if he had been born in 1767. As it is unlikely that he remained active in the printing business after reaching the age of 100, placing his date of birth in the 1770s is probably the best and most reasonable estimate.

2   "Catherine Goadson, Theft." *The Proceedings of the Old Bailey*, April 2013, accessed 17th October 2014. http://www.oldbaileyonline.org/browse.jsp?div=t17670715-17

3   Ian Maxted. "Exeter Working Papers in British Book Trade History; 0 The London book trades 1775-1800: a preliminary checklist of members. Names R." *Exeter Working papers in Book History*, 11th January 2007, accessed 17th October 2014.

http://bookhistory.blogspot.co.uk/2007/01/london-1775-1800-r.html

4   Janet M. Todd. *Jane Austen in context*. Cambridge: Cambridge University Press, 2005. Page 199.

5   Kathryn Sutherland. *Jane Austin's Textual Lives*. Oxford: Oxford University Press, 2005. Page 164.

6   J.D. Aylward. *The English Master of Arms*. London: Routledge & Kegan Paul, 1956. Page 219.

7   Keith Farrell. *Scottish Broadsword and British Singlestick*. Glasgow: Fallen Rook Publishing, 2014. Pages 115-117.

8   J.D. Aylward. *The English Master of Arms*. London: Routledge & Kegan Paul, 1956. Page 214.

9   J.D. Aylward. *The English Master of Arms*. London: Routledge & Kegan Paul, 1956. Page 219.

10 Keith Farrell. *Scottish Broadsword and British Singlestick*. Glasgow: Fallen Rook Publishing, 2014. Page 91.

11 J.D. Aylward. *The English Master of Arms*. London: Routledge & Kegan Paul, 1956. Page 219.

12 "Henry Roworth." *MyHeritage Genealogy*, accessed 18th October 2014. http://www.myheritage. com/research/collection-1/myheritage-family-trees?itemId=171873012-4-2276&action=showRecord

13 Elizabeth Janson. "Australian Pioneer Families." *Australian Pioneer Families*, 26th January 2005, accessed 18th October 2014. http://www.oocities.org/mepnab/r/r40.html#roworth

14 Ian Maxted. "Exeter Working Papers in British Book Trade History; 0 The London book trades 1775-1800: a preliminary checklist of members. Names R." *Exeter Working papers in Book History*, 11th January 2007, accessed 17th October 2014.

http://bookhistory.blogspot.co.uk/2007/01/london-1775-1800-r.html

15 Walter Arthur Copinger. *The Law of Copyright, in Works of Literature and Art*. Clark, NJ: The Lawbook Exchange, 2012. Page ix.

16 Charles Henry Timperley. *A Dictionary of Printers and Printing*. London: H. Johnson, 1839. Page 832.

17 Ronan Deazley. *Rethinking Copyright: History, Theory, Language*. Cheltenham: Edward Elgar Publishing, 2006. Page 35.

18 Keith Farrell. *Scottish Broadsword and British Singlestick*. Glasgow: Fallen Rook Publishing, 2014. Page 94.

19 "Thomas Wilson, Theft." *The Proceedings of the Old Bailey*, April 2013, accessed 17th October 2014. http://www.oldbaileyonline.org/browse.jsp?div=t18310217-190

20 Ian Maxted. "Exeter Working Papers in British Book Trade History; 0 The London book trades 1775-1800: a preliminary checklist of members. Names R." *Exeter Working papers in Book History*, 11th January 2007, accessed 17th October 2014.

http://bookhistory.blogspot.co.uk/2007/01/london-1775-1800-r.html

21 Center for Applied Technologies in the Humanities. "Charles Roworth." *Lord Byron and his Times*, accessed 17th October 2014. http://lordbyron.cath.lib.vt.edu/persRec.php?choose=PersRefs&selectPerson=ChRowor1869

22 "Notice." *The London Gazette*. 23rd August, 1872. Page 3788.

23 "Henry Roworth." *MyHeritage Genealogy*, accessed 18th October 2014. http://www.myheritage. com/research/collection-1/myheritage-family-trees?itemId=171873012-4-2276&action=showRecord

THE

ART OF DEFENCE ON FOOT

WITH THE

Broad Sword and Sabre,

UNITING

The SCOTCH and AUSTRIAN METHODS

INTO

ONE REGULAR SYSTEM.

TO WHICH ARE ADDED

REMARKS ON THE SPADROON.

LONDON:

PRINTED FOR T. EGERTON, AT THE MILITARY
LIBRARY, NEAR WHITEHALL.

1798.

CONTENTS.

PART I.

PRACTICE at the TARGET.

PART

[2]

PART II.

PRACTICE with ANTAGONIST.

APPLI-

[3]

APPLICATION of the POINT.

APPENDIX.

THE

ART OF DEFENCE

WITH THE

BROAD SWORD AND SABRE.

THE following treatife is divided into Two
Parts. The FIRST containing a *Mode of
Practice at a Target**, which may frequently afford
exercife or amufement when it may not be poffible, at the inftant, to find another perfon equally
defirous of improvement in the fcience. In this
part is defcribed the Auftrian method of directing
the edge, and recovering to a guard from any cut

---

* The target for this purpofe will be found at the beginning of the book, from whence it may be taken and fixed
againft a wall or partition, as directed in p. 11.

which

which may have either miffed or cut through its object, without fuffering your body to remain exposed, or ftraining your wrift.

It is not, however, neceffary for learners to occupy a great length of time with the firft part, before they proceed to practife with an antagonift: it will be fufficient if they make themfelves acquainted with the direction of the feveral cuts and the numbers by which they are diftinguifhed: the mode of recovering to guard by whirling up the blade, and the turns of the wrift requifite for that purpofe, may be acquired at convenient intervals, by practifing with either a fabre, broad fword, cut and thruft fword, or hanger, and gentlemen will by that means become accuftomed to the weight of the weapon, and accurate in carrying a true edge ; whereas if they practife *only* with a ftick, the weight of the fword will render it fo unwieldy when they are compelled to draw it on a real occafion, as to fruftrate almoft every offenfive movement made againft an antagonift poffeffed of either fcience or agility.

The

The SECOND PART treats of the *Practice with an Antagonist*; by attention to which gentlemen may improve each other very faſt, provided they act and communicate their remarks, as directed under the head of GENERAL OBSERVATIONS, p. 31, with that candour which every one has a right to expect in this kind of friendly conteſt and amuſement.

I would not however venture to recommend the practice with a friend for the ſake of improvement with naked ſwords; ſince although not attended with danger in the cavalry exerciſe, yet as the ſituation of perſons engaged on foot does not confine them to one or two particular cuts at commencing the attack, but admits of more various and complicated movements, an error in regard to the parades might prove fatal.

In this treatiſe the broad ſword and ſabre are generally mentioned, yet the inſtructions will be found equally applicable to the hanger and ſpadroon,

droon, or light cut and thruſt ſword. The deviations which may prove neceſſary for the latter are
noticed under the head of REMARKS on the SPA-
DROON.

In the APPENDIX are ſome hints which may
be found uſeful when oppoſing a perſon armed
with a ſmall ſword, or with a muſquet and bayonet.
The variations from the general principles of the
ſyſtem, when contending with ſticks only, are
alſo noticed in that part.

PART

PART I.

PRACTICE AT THE TARGET.

―――――――

Of HOLDING the SWORD or SABRE.

THE broad fword and fabre muft be held with
the fingers and thumb clenched round the
gripe, fufficiently faft to prevent the blade wavering. At the inftant of parrying or attacking, it
will be requifite to grafp it with ftrength, but
that exertion of the mufcles is fo natural, as not
to need much infifting on. The chief object is
to keep the gripe encircled as much as poffible
with the fore-finger and thumb, whatever may
be the pofition of the blade, relaxing or contracting the other fingers according to its direction.
Placing the thumb upon the back of the gripe
(as is the cafe with the fmall fword) can feldom, if ever, be of fervice when ufing the broad

B   fword,

fword, and the curve of the fabre blade renders
it unmanageable and unfteady if held in that manner. In practifing with light fticks the placing
the thumb in that pofition may be found to give
a celerity and fharpnefs to the cut, yet the weight
of the blade of either a broad fword or fabre, will
prove too great to be acted upon in a fimilar manner, while the perfon thus holding his weapon
will be liable to be difarmed, if oppofed by a forcible ftroke from one of equal ftrength.

METHOD

POSITION.

THE firſt object of the learner ſhould be to attain a firm yet flexible poſition. For this purpoſe he muſt learn to ſupport the moſt part, if not the whole, of his weight on his *left* leg, in order that the right, which is to be advanced, may be either retired from a cut, or thrown rapidly forward on a lunge. It is therefore neceſſary to commence the practice in the following manner.

Fix the ſheet, on which the ſix cuts are deſcribed, flat to the wall, the center of it about one inch below the height of your ſhoulder. Leading to the perpendicular line down the center, mark a line with chalk on the floor. At the diſtance of about ten feet from the figure place your left heel ſo as juſt to touch the line, the left knee bent, to throw the weight of the body on that leg, the right foot advanced about 14 or 16 inches towards the target; the toe pointing to the perpendicular line. The left ſhoulder muſt be thrown back, and the

B 2   body

body kept as much in a line as poffible, in order
to expofe no more of it than neceffary to your fuppofed antagonift. The left hand may be held up
within about fix inches of the left ear, in order to
preferve the balance of the body; or may be fixed
firm with the infide of it on the left hip bone, as
may be found moft convenient.

From the above pofition, practife flipping the
right foot back till the middle of it becomes oppofite the left heel, in order to retire the right
knee from your adverfary's reach when neceffary,
which is eafily and quickly done, if you reft no
more weight than directed on that foot.

LUNGING

IS the ftepping forth with the right foot from the
pofition defcribed in the preceding page, in order to effect a cut or thruft. In beginning this
practice, make the firft trial without attempting a cut at the fame time, till you can lunge
straight

ftraight upon the line on the floor, keeping your left foot firm, and recover yourfelf with eafe.

At the inftant of lunging, the left hand fhould drop on the left thigh; from whence it fhould be thrown up fmartly above the left ear as you reco-ver, which will affift in regaining your pofition.

Although an extenfive lunge is doubtlefs advan-tageous to thofe who can make it eafily, yet it will not be found on a real occafion fo neceffary as a quick recover. For which reafon it will be im-prudent in gentlemen to accuftom themfelves to ftep farther out than their ftrength or activity na-turally admit. Care muft always be taken to place the right foot flat on the ground, and not to make fo violent an extenfion, as to pitch on the heel of that foot.* The proper extent is to bring the left knee ftraight and the right knee perpendicular to the inftep.

---

* It fhould be confidered that in real conteft the differ-ence of the ground, and many other circumftances, concur to render any unneceffary extenfion hazardous; efpecially to fuch perfons as have ufed themfelves to practife on an even floor, perhaps with flippers chalked at the bottom

After

After practifing the lunge until you are enabled to ftep well forward and recover without difficulty, the next object is to execute the cuts in fuch a manner as not to expofe yourfelf to a counter or retort, by fuffering your arm to fway improperly with the motion of your fword.

To prevent accidents, by the fword efcaping from the hand, it will be neceffary to have a lea-ther fword knot, which fhould be foft and pliable, and not fo tight as to confine the motion of the wrift.

Before you draw the fword, pafs your hand through the loop, and give it a couple of turns in-wards, which will render it fufficiently fecure.

As all attacks fhould be preceded by a defenfive pofture, and concluded by a return to one, it may be neceffary to commence with the following guards, from whence the cuts are chiefly made. I fhall referve the defcription of the others until I treat on the practice with an antagonift.

MEDIUM

MEDIUM GUARD.

THIS pofition rather merits the appellation of *prepare to guard*, as it affords hardly any protection without fome change of pofition, and fhould be only adopted (if at all) when you are in doubt on which fide your adverfary means to join, and before his weapon is within reach of yours. It confifts in prefenting your fword per-pendicular, with the fhell oppofite the bottom of the target, the point upwards, and the edge op-pofite the line down the middle.

It muft be obferved as an invariable rule, that the ward-iron fhould be exactly over the middle knuckles, either when holding a guard or making a cut, by which means the direction of the knuckles will always govern the edge of the weapon.

INSIDE

INSIDE GUARD.

FROM the medium guard, by a turn of the wrist, bring the hilt of the sword opposite A, the finger nails upwards, the blade sloping sufficiently acrofs the target to direct the point to C, the arm straight from the shoulder to the wrist, but not too stiff.

In this position the edge of the sword is to receive the blow from an antagonist, and the bevel of the blade next the edge should be opposite to the dotted line from A to C. If you turn the edge too much to the left, you will find a difficulty in striking, or be exposed to a cut on the outside of the wrist.

This guard secures the face and front of the body from cuts I. and V.

OUTSIDE

OUTSIDE GUARD.

FROM the laſt deſcribed poſition, by a motion of the wriſt turn your knuckles outward till the hilt arrives oppoſite **B**, the blade at the ſame inſtant croſſing the target till the point is directed to **D**, the arm extended and ſtraight: the bevel of the edge oppoſite the dotted line from **B** to **D**, and the finger nails downwards.

Having obſerved the relative ſituation of theſe two guards, practiſe the change from one to the other and back again, till you are able to execute it with ſuch agility and preciſion, as to render it impoſſible for an adverſary to diſengage his weapon from one ſide and cut at the other without being oppoſed by the edge of your ſword.

In this parade, the action of the wriſt ſhould always precede that of the ſhoulder; and be

so immediately followed by it, as not to prefent
an opening to your adverfary by holding a crooked
wrift; an error to which beginners are very liable,
efpecially on the infide guard.

INTRODUCTORY REMARKS *on the* SIX CUTS.

THE following method of making the fix cuts
though not practifed or taught as a neceffary
part of the fcience of broad fword in England, till
lately introduced into the cavalry exercife, will be
found attended with many advantages. For inftance: when firft engaging, many perfons are
apt to retire out of diftance as you aim the firft or
fecond ftroke, if they have fufficient fpace for that
purpofe, and unlefs fuch cut be made on a principle of expeditioufly recovering your weapon, the
lofs of time will afford your antagonift an opportunity of cutting or thrufting before you regain

your

your defensive posture. Others practise a mode
of slipping a cut by withdrawing the arm; in
which if they succeed, they are almost certain of
throwing in a cut before you can recover from a
forcible stroke, unless you have accustomed yourself to this manner of executing the six cuts.

Secondly. The strain, from the weight of your
sword and force of the blow, may so far disable
your wrist, as to render you incapable either of a
vigorous attack or of a quick and firm parade.

On which account a person who cannot perform
the cuts upon the principle here recommended,
must not attempt to strike with rapidity or force,
until he perceive an absolute certainty of every
blow reaching his antagonist unless parried by his
weapon.

This disadvantage is obviated by the following
method of practice; in addition to which, facility
of execution and flexibility of wrist are obtained.

In

In making cuts I. and II. the point nearly de-
scribes a circle, from the commencement of the
cut to the return to the guard :—To make this
easily from the motion of the wrist and preserve
the arm in its proper direction is of much impor-
tance, and can only be attained *by beginning*
gradually, and observing how far you can conduct
the blade in making the cut' in the requisite di-
rection, without straining the wrist, or disordering
your position. For instance, in making cut I.
you will find that you cannot proceed farther than
to bring your point a little below fig. 4, without
some change of position: this change must be
effected by turning the wrist, till you can give free-
dom to the blade to complete the remainder of the
circle, which brings the point up to the front of
your position. Every unnecessary width of motion (which would be a sure consequence of
bending the arm) must be avoided. Therefore,
having brought your point from fig. 1 to fig. 4 in
the first attempt, pause and observe the position
necessary to be taken by the wrist, as described in
the directions for making cut I.

A similar

bringing up the blade with a fweep clear of the infide (or front) of your pofition.

———

CUT II.

Motion 1. FROM the infide guard, turn your knuckles towards B, the point of your fword to fig. 2.

Motion 2. Conduct the point of the fword from 2 to 3.

Motion 3. Turn the infide of the wrift upwards, which will drop the point of the fword outwards to the rear, relax the three fingers neareft the pummel, and recover to the outfide guard by raifing the blade with a fweep clear of the right fhoulder.

C   Having

Having afcertained the changes of the wrift neceffary to recover your blade in thefe two cuts, practife them until you are able to perform each as one motion without any paufe, and to recover from either cut to the infide or outfide guard as occafion may require.

CUT III.

Motion 1. BY turning the upper part of the wrift and back of the hand downwards from the infide guard, drop the point outwards to the right till the edge of the blade is oppofite the diagonal line from 3. to 2. at the fame inftant raifing the wrift with a ftraight arm as high as the fhoulder.

Motion 2. By the contraction of the fingers and motion of the wrift conduct the point up the line from 3 to 2.

When

Motion 3. When arrived at fig. 2. turn the back of the hand up, and drop the hand fo as to bring the blade into the pofition of the outfide guard.

CUT IV.

Motion 1. FROM the outfide guard by a turn of the wrift, drop the point to the left, till the edge becomes oppofite the diagonal line from 4. to 1. raifing your hand to the height of your fhoulder, the arm extended and ftraight.

Motion 2. By the fpring of the wrift conduct the point along the line from 4. to 1.

Motion 3. Turn the infide of the wrift rather upwards, and finking the arm, come to the infide guard.

CUT

CUT V.

Motion 1. TURN the back of the hand downward from the infide guard, thereby dropping the point of the fword to
the right till it becomes oppofite fig. 5.

Motion 2. By inclining the wrift inward, and
keeping the nails upward, the point will
be conducted acrofs the target to fig. 6.

Motion 3. Raife the point from fig. 6. to C. and
come to the infide guard.

CUT VI.

IS the reverfe of cut V. and is performed with
the nails downward.

Motion 1. Drop the point to the left till oppofite
fig. 6.

Motion

Motion 2.   By inclining the wrift outwards make
the cut acrofs the target to fig. 5.

Motion 3.   Raife the point to D, and recover to
the outfide guard.

═══════════

COMBINING *the* SIX CUTS.

I T will be now proper fo to combine the preceding fix cuts, that they may all be performed without paufing, which will be found extremely ufeful in an attack, efpecially if your antagonift breaks ground and continues to retire, as
is frequently the cafe at the onfet; it may alfo
prove advantageous in an engagement at night;
fince if properly performed, the blade will necefla-
rily crofs your own pofition in fuch manner as to
afford confiderable fecurity from the ftroke of your
adverfary, and by the reiterated attack will compel
him to remain almoft entirely on the defenfive, or
fubject him to a certainty of receiving your edge
on his fword arm, particularly if he does not

know

know the direction of thofe cuts which fo rapidly fucceed the one he may have at firft efcaped or parried.

The difference between executing the fix cuts fingly as before defcribed and when combined, confifts in not reforting to any particular guard after each cut, but continuing your attack from cut I. till you have made II. III. IV. V. and VI. in doing which the point proceeds from the con- clufion of one cut to the commencement of the next, according to the dotted lines on the plate.

Be cautious not to lift your arm towards the figure at which the cut begins, as that would leave your body unprotected.

PART

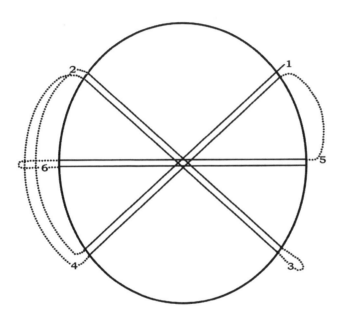

The Six Cuts.

PART II.

PRACTICE with ANTAGONIST.

═══════════

GENERAL OBSERVATIONS.

IN commencing your practice with an antagonist, for the fake of improvement, begin flowly: the one taking the defensive part entirely; the other attacking, and mentioning the number of the cut he means to make; each carefully obferving the motion of his opponent, and informing him what part appears to become expofed by the changes from one pofition to another; where any defeét of that kind appears, repeat your praétice till by the correétnefs or celerity thus acquired, you become more perfeét. Then change fituations, and let the affailant aét on the defenfive. By making obfervations coolly in this manner, you will acquire more fkill and precifion in one leffon, than in playing twenty at random; and will likewife avoid unpleafant accidents.

Next proceed to attack and defend without
naming what cuts you intend; in doing which endeavour firſt to become correct in making cuts I.
and II. and oppoſing them by the inſide and outſide guards. Then add III and IV. Afterwards,
V. and VI. encreaſing the celerity of your attack
by degrees, and oppoſing each cut according to
the following table.

Cut I. Oppoſed by *Inſide Guard*, deſcribed in p. 50

II. ———— *Outſide Guard* . . 53

III. { if made at the body. } *Inſide Guard*, 2d poſition 51

III. { if made at the wriſt. } *Inſide Guard*, 3d poſition 52

IV. ———— *Hanging Guard* . 54

V. ———— *Inſide Guard* , . 50

VI. ———— *Outſide Guard* . 53

or *Hanging Guard* . 54

Cuts made directly at the head are oppoſed by

the *St. George* 58

The whole of the ſix cuts may be warded by the
hanging guard, the hand or blade being moved a
little

little to right or left, and raised or lowered ac-
cordingly: but obferve, if already engaged on
an *infide guard*, it will be ufelefs to attempt taking
the hanging guard againſt Cut V. or III.

I have before remarked that it will be unfafe
in friendly practice to make ufe of naked broad
fwords or fabres, and ſhall now take the liberty of
cautioning learners, who wiſh to attain the fcience
of real defence, alfo againſt the falfe mode of de-
fending themfelves with a baſket fo large as that
which cudgel players generally ufe, and on which
they receive two thirds of the blows aimed at them,
fince that will be accuſtoming themfelves to a protection which they cannot have on a real occafion.

The baſkets for this purpofe ſhould therefore be
made narrow, and as fmall as poſſible without hurt-
ing the hand: and as gentlemen ſhould always endeavour to defend themfelves rather with the *fort
of the fword than the hilt, they ought not to prac-

* The *fort* of the fword is that half of the blade next the
hilt; the half neareſt the point is denominated the *feeble*.

tife

ufe ftopping a blow with the fides, or any other part of the bafket except where the hilt of a fword would equally projeft.

By marking a narrow line with chalk down the fuppofed edge of the ftick, accuracy in carrying the edge of the fword may be acquired.

In part I. the *mode of recovering to guard* has been confidered under the idea of the cuts not meeting with fufficient refiftance either from the blade or body of your antagonift to impede their courfe: but in practifing with an opponent, it is not to be underftood that the recovery to guard muft be *always* made on that principle: From cuts I. and II. when parried, the blade naturally rebounds up the line in which it fell, till the point rifes high enough to form an infide or outfide guard. From cuts V. and VI. the point muft be raifed in a fimilar manner, if the cut is oppofed by the blade of your antagonift. In making cuts III. and IV. it fhould be a rule, never to apply above four inches of the point, in order that it may free

itfelf

itfelf, and mount to the infide or outfide guard : if that be prevented by your antagonift's blade croffing above yours, you muft withdraw your blade from your attempt to make cut IiI. under the fpadroon guard, and from attempting cut IV. under the hanging guard.

After making a cut be careful always to recover to that guard which brings your *edge* oppofed to your antagonift's blade.

If at any time you fhould be compelled to op-pofe a weak parade to your adverfary, by your wrift being in a conftrained pofition, quit that pof-ture as foon as poffible, either by directing a cut at him, or fpringing back at the inftant you change.

To attain fecurity from a counter ftroke whilft at-tacking, it is requifite that in every cut made by you the fort of your fword fhould be directed in fome degree towards your antagonift's weapon, fo that although the point of your fword may ef-fect the cut, yet the fort fhall at the fame inftant be oppofed to any blow he may then deliver. For example :

In

In making cut I., the hilt being carried to the
left of your pofition, as much as when on the infide guard, at the inftant the point commences the
cut, occafions your blade to form a crofs on that
of your antagonift, and thereby affords a certainty
of protection, unlefs he can change his pofition
confiderably in lefs time than you can make the
cut. Cuts I. and II. fhould therefore in general
be made with the hand lower than the fhoulder,
and III. and IV. with it raifed above the height
of the fhoulder,

On this principle it is that the ARM *fhould never*
be lifted towards the fide at which you intend a
cut, fince by that motion both hilt and blade would
be entirely removed from between yourfelf and
antagonift, and confequently you muft become
expofed to the fame cut you aim at him.

Experience will foon direct to how great a degree it is requifite thus to crofs your adverfary's
blade. By extending the principle to an unneceffary extreme, you may indeed frequently prevent

vent your own blow taking effect, by encountering your antagonift's fword only; and, on the other hand, by not fufficiently obferving it, may become expofed yourfelf by every cut you attempt.

In fome fituations it will undoubtedly be proper to cut *from* your antagonift's blade, inftead of *towards* it; for inftance in making a cut over and within his guard, or under and within his guard; in fuch cafes this attack may be fafely rifqued, becaufe you have previoufly forced his fword far enough from the line to prevent a counter ftroke or retort before your recover takes place.

DISTANCE.

WANT of attention to preferve the proper diftance is an error to which beginners are very liable. No invariably pofitive fpace can be recommended, as almoft every fituation muft depend on the height, ftrength and activity of your opponent. The moft general principle that can be laid down is, that your left knee fhould be about

three

three inches beyond the reach of your antagonist's point upon the most extensive lunge he can exert. But it is difficult to prove your distance by this method in real contest; in that case you may judge more easily from the point of your sword just reaching his shell when both your arms are straight, and neither inclining the body improperly forward. If you permit him to advance nearer, he may throw in a cut or thrust too rapidly for your parade, especially if he first deceive you by a feint. To avoid this, some persons accustom themselves to spring back, frequently dropping their point to their antagonist's face, when contending with one of an impetuous and forward temper; a mode which will undoubtedly be found very useful, if the ground on which they are engaged should afford sufficient room.——Others adopt a circular step to right or left, and thereby effect their purpose in less length. But experience and practice will best determine which to make use of, according to the circumstances and situation in which you may chance to contend.

The

The ADVANCE.

IS to gain ground upon an adverfary when at too
great a diftance to reach him by a lunge, or by
preffing forwards to compel him to retreat into worfe
ground or a more difadvantageous fituation : it is
effected by ftepping forward with the right foot
about one third of your lunge, at the fame time
transferring the weight of your body from the
left leg to the right, that you may be enabled to
flip the left foot along the ground to within fix
inches of the right heel; then ftep forward again
with the right foot, and draw up the left as before
(ftill preferving the pofition of body erect, and being careful to oppofe a proper guard) till your object be attained.

The RETREAT

IS ufed to gain a more advantageous fituation
that may be behind you, or to avoid any in-
convenience you may fuftain from an adverfary of
fuperior ftrength or impetuous temper preffing too
clofely upon you. In this fituation the left leg muft
lead, and the weight be thrown in the firft motion
on the right, lifting the left foot from the ground
to avoid any unfeen obftacle in the rear, then
planting it firmly about fixteen or eighteen inches
backward, and drawing the right to within ten.
After this raife the left foot, and planting it as before, draw the right after it, continuing your retreat
as occafion may require.

TRA-

TRAVERSING.

THERE are two modes of traverfing, viz. *backward* and *forward*; either of which may be adopted according to the ground or other circumftances in which you may engage, and will be found ufeful, if in retiring from an adverfary you are obftructed by a ditch or other impediment. Traverfing is preferred to retiring by many, becaufe it has not fo much the appearance of fuffering a defeat.

The FORE TRAVERSE

IS performed in a large circle, the center of which is the middle of the *line of defence,** on which line you and your adverfary engage, fuch

---

* A ftraight line fuppofed to be drawn through the center of your own body and that of your adverfary, which fhould be the center of motion to your body, and in the very middle of every guard and every cut.

D is

is the line P, Q, C, H, G, in the oppofite page, and the circle formed by the traverfe will be P, A, C, E, G, I, L, N: For the right foot being at Q and the left at P, the traverfe is begun by ftepping about with the left foot from P to A, and the right foot immediately after from Q to B; and then the line A, B, C, K, I, will be the line of defence; at the next ftep remove the left foot from A to C, then the right from B to D; which will make the line C, D, C, M, L, the line of defence. In the fame manner continue till you have obviated your difficulty, or drawn your antagonift into the bad ground, carefully attending to your guard, and not ftepping fo far as to diforder the erect pofition of your body.

The BACK TRAVERSE

IS the counter-part of that already defcribed; and is commenced by moving the *right* foot firft: for inftance: Standing in the line of defence P, Q, C, H, G, remove the right from Q to O, the

left

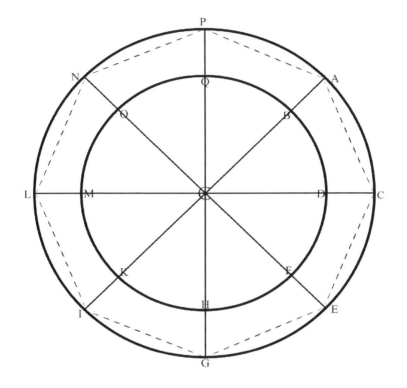

Traverse.

from from ʀ to ɴ, which renders the line ɴ, o, C, ꜰ, ᴇ, the line of defence: Thus ſtepping back, the right foot moving firſt, you may traverſe the whole or ſuch part of the circle as may be requiſite.

This practice may at times prove exceedingly uſeful, eſpecially if you ſhould be at firſt engaged with the ſun directly in your face, as a perſon who performs it readily, by traverſing half the circle, brings his opponent into the place he has juſt quitted, and by a vigorous attack at that inſtant may redouble the embarraſſment.

DIS-

DISENGAGING

CONSISTS in quitting that fide of your antagonift's blade on which you are oppofed by
his guard, in order to effect a cut or thruft where
an opportunity may prefent. It is performed
either by raifing the point of your fword towards
yourfelf fo as juft fufficiently to clear the blade of
your opponent, or by dropping the point below
his hilt. The change in either way fhould be
made very quickly, and in the inftant of paffing
your adverfary's weapon, the edge of your blade
fhould be turned to meet any cut that he may direct at you, otherwife you become liable to be dif-
abled, from the ward-iron not protecting the hand.

The difengage to effect a cut is generally performed over the wrift; that with intention of
thrufting, under it. To cut III. or IV. under the
wrift, it is fometimes beft to difengage below it.

FORCING

FORCING *your* ADVERSARY's BLADE.

IF at any time your antagonift appears languid and weak on his guard, and barely covers his body on the fide he is oppofed; by ftepping well forward and ftriking your fort fmartly on his blade, you may be enabled to deliver a cut without rifk even at the part he intends to fecure, taking care to direct your blade in fuch a manner that the plate or crofs bar of your hilt fhall prevent his fword coming forward, and fufficiently bearing your hand to the fide oppofite that at which your point is directed, to prevent an interchanged cut.

This fhould be performed partly by the fudden extenfion of the arm, and partly by the fpring of the wrift.

TIMING

TIMING

IS the exact and critical throwing in a cut or thruft upon any opening that may occur as your antagonift changes his pofition. For inftance, if he changes from an infide to an outfide guard, or from outfide to infide, in a negligent manner, his wrift becomes expofed, and frequently part of his fword arm above the elbow. The fame opportunity prefents itfelf, if in his feints he fhould fuffer his fword to fway his arm, inftead of making them lightly from his wrift, or fhould not recover quickly from a cut which you have parried.

The SLIP

IS performed by withdrawing that part at which your antagonift directs his cut; in order that his weapon being deprived of the expected refiftance may fway his arm from the defenfive pofture, and thereby afford an opening for a cut. It will

not

not however often effect this purpose againft a perfon who can execute the cuts on the principle recommended in this work, as the recovery is fo
very expeditious; but may prove an excellent de-
ception againft an impetuous antagonift, efpecially
if he be ignorant of the fcience.*

It will therefore be proper for the learner to accuftom himfelf fometimes to recover from the lunge
with his right hand drawn quickly up to the breaft,
the edge of his fword turned to the left or right,
according to the direction of the cut he means to
flip. If the cut he intends to avoid be made at the
infide of the fword arm, the edge fhould be turned
to the left as in the infide guard, and the point

* It has been frequently afferted, that a bold active man,
unacquainted with the art, by rufhing forward with repeated
attacks, will perplex a good fwordfman, and, if not defeat
him, reduce the conteft to an equal hazard; but this can
only happen if fuch fwordfman has never reflected on the
meafures fit to be adopted in an engagement of that nature.
For inftance, if a fwordfman flips a cut attempted by one
of that defcription, inftead of parrying it, he may effect a
cut before the ignorant can poffibly recover, and with fuch
force as totally to deprive his antagonift of that vigour and
audacity on which alone he could depend.

D 4   raifed

raifed perpendicular to the hilt, and the return from this pofition fhould be cut II. Should the attack be made at the outfide of his arm, the edge fhould be turned outwards, and the hilt held a little below the right fhoulder, returning cut I. the inftant his adverfary's blade paffes ; but this latter pofition is neither fo practicable nor fafe as the former, and in general requires, that the right foot fhould be retired as well as the arm, which lengthens the time of motion, and will frequently prevent you from throwing in a cut quick enough.

Some are fo partial to this manœuvre of flipping an adverfary's cut, that by practice they become enabled to flip a cut even when directed at their body. But this, unlefs exceedingly well executed, becomes hazardous, on account of its difordering their pofition, efpecially if an adverfary fhould lunge farther than expected, and cut low; added to which, by throwing their body from the line of defence, the antagonift may be induced to thruft upon them in that unguarded pofition, and will thereby obtain a decided advantage.

In

In circumſtances where the withdrawing the hand up to the breaſt is not ſufficient, the ſlipping a cut on the inſide is effected by drawing the right foot backward and ſideways to the right of the line, letting your adverſary's ſword paſs a little out of reach, then ſtepping into the former poſition, return cut II. or VI. at his outſide, which becomes expoſed by his weapon not meeting the reſiſtance expected.

To an outſide cut the ſlip is performed by drawing the right leg with the whole body backwards and ſideways a ſmall degree out of the line towards the left, contracting the arm a little, the ſword ſtill in the line, and under an outſide guard; let your antagoniſt's point paſs, and returning your right foot to its former place, make cut I. at the inſide of the arm, or II. at the head. I have mentioned this method of performing the outſide ſlip, as it is attempted by ſome, but not with intention of recommending it, as the hazard is much greater than the probable advantage.

On

On the hanging guard the flip may be practifed
with great fafety, by ftepping the foot quite out
of and at right angles with the line of defence, the
whole body being thus brought well beyond it
toward the right; and the guard remaining ftill
oppofed to your antagonift to protect you from
his cut, in cafe he fhould lunge farther than you
expect.

INSIDE GUARD.

TURN your hilt as much to the left of your
position as when practifing at the target; the
pummel oppofite your right breaft, the finger nails
upwards, the point of your fword elevated 6 or 8
inches above the head of your antagonift, and as
near in a line perpendicular to his left eye as poffible. Should your antagonift bear againft your
blade to force it out of the line, raife your point,
fo as to withdraw your feeble from his bearing;
or difengage quickly and cut at the outfide of his
arm.

Cut

Inside Guard.

Pub.ᵈ as the act directs by T.Egerton Military Library Whitehall.

Inside Guard 2.ᵈ Position.

Pub.ᵈ as the act directs by I. Egerton Military Library Whitehall.

Cuts L and V. are warded by this position, the latter however requires a trifling inclination of the hand downwards.

In parrying cut I. at the cheek, it will be found advisable to carry the wrist rather more to the left, raising the point nearly perpendicular, to prevent you from being deceived by a feint:—If you suffer your point to remain low, an offer may be made at your cheek, and the cut delivered over your guard at the head.

INSIDE GUARD, 2d *Position.*

SHOULD your antagonist attempt cut III. at the inside of the body, you may parry it by sinking your hand towards your left knee, directing your point towards his face, and withdrawing the right leg sufficiently behind the left to preserve your balance. Be cautious not to remain in this position, as it exposes the upper part of the arm and body.

If

If your antagonist fhould have advanced near
enough to direct the cut at your thigh, you muft
fink well on both knees, in order to lower your
hilt fufficiently.

INSIDE GUARD, *3d Pofition.*

WHEN cut III. is made at the wrift, it will
be only requifite to meet your adverfary's
blade with your fort or ward-iron, by turning
down your knuckles and directing your point to
the left, finking your hand towards your right hip.
This will alfo parry it when aimed at the body.

Cut III. when made at the wrift may alfo be
flipped by drawing the hand up to the breaft, in
which cafe you obtain an opening at the outfide of
your antagonift's fword-arm.

OUTSIDE

Outside Guard.

Pub. as the act directs by I.Egerton Military Library Whitehall.

OUTSIDE GUARD.

TURN your knuckles to the outfide as when practifing at the target, your nails downwards, your point elevated about 6 or 8 inches above the head of your antagonift, in a line perpendicular with his right eye. Should he endeavour to force your blade out of the pofition, gain his feeble by withdrawing and raifing your point,* or difengage and cut on the other fide.

This guard fecures againft cut II. and by finking the hand in a fmall degree, againft cut VI.

* If your adverfary's point has croffed above the back of your blade fo as threaten the infide of your pofition, adopt the hanging guard, by throwing up your wrift quickly as poffible, and bear his blade off to the infide; fhould you attempt to parry by the outfide guard after his point has croffed your blade in fuch a degree as to come withinfide your guard, you will only add to the force of his cut. See cut V *over and within the guard*, p. 81.

HANGING

HANGING GUARD.

THIS pofition may be taken from the *infide* or *outfide guard*, by dropping the point of your fword a little above your antagonift's right hip, the edge towards him, raifing the hand as high as your head, and looking your adverfary in the face under the fhell of your fword; your arm extended and perfectly ftraight : or it may be adopted immediately on drawing your fword, by raifing your hand and extending your arm as above.

When in this pofition, the adverfary's fword muft be kept by your blade fufficiently to the outfide to prevent any cut or thruft being made at that part; which forms what is termed the *Seconde Hanging Guard*, and fecures you from cuts II. IV. and VI. When ufed to parry a thruft it will feldom be neceffary to raife the hand higher than the fhoulder.

If your antagonift difengages from the above to make cuts I. III. or V. you muft oppofe them by

the

g the advantages to be derived from the guard, the moſt important will be found rotection it affords by covering ſo large of the body, as the whole of the blade priated to that purpoſe, eſpecially in the di- in which the firſt and moſt natural blows e; while from the oblique poſition of the a blow, however forcible, ſlides down out endangering the hand. For theſe it ſeems well calculated to parry off any attack in the dark, eſpecially if it ſhould be gainſt a perſon armed only with a ſtick.

hanging guard is alſo well adapted to pre- antagoniſt from thruſting at the body beneath ſt, and to obviate thoſe feints which might iſe be made, by ſhifting his point from ſide under your wriſt on either the inſide or guard.

ther material advantage is, that it requires trifling motion of the wriſt to meet with blade any cut whatever that may be made.

The

Seconde Hanging Guard.

Pub.ᵈ as the act directs by T.Egerton Military Library Whitehall.

the *Prime Hanging*
clining your wrift t
hand is in a line al
ther lowered, to pre
it.   This pofition is
as the other, and fl
cuts above mentione

It will be neceffar
gree of firmnefs and
prime to the *feconde*
made at either of th
failant's fword to reb
bles him without m
other fide. *

The hanging guard
and is at the fame time
fhall mention the prir
learner to exercife his
cumftances to adopt it

* It is againft the rules
or friendly contefts, to m
in an engagement for life
to; therefore the learner fhe

Amon
hanging
in the
a portio
is appro
rection
are mad
weapon
it with
reafons,
fudden
made a

The
vent an
the wri
otherw
to fide
outfid

An
a very
your

The chief objection arifes from the difficulty of attacking from it, as you can hardly make any cut except cut IV. and VI. without expofing your-felf, and thofe cuts exceedingly weak, owing to the want of fweep to give force to the blade. In making every other cut, the blade muft defert the part it fhould protect; and having fo great a portion of the circle to defcribe, the wrift at the fame time being much elevated, you are liable to a counter-ftroke from your adverfary, if he remain on the infide guard watching an opportunity.

The conftrained pofition of the hand and weight of the weapon will at firft be found tirefome on this guard, but practice will foon overcome that defect, and enable a perfon to deliver a blow with amazing rapidity and force from it, as may be ob-ferved in the practice of the French Spadroon players, many of whom place their chief depen-dence on the protection afforded by their guard in feconde, which only differs from this guard in the wrift not being held quite fo high.

E

St.

St. GEORGE's GUARD

IS intended to ward a blow at the top of the head, if your adverfary difengages from the outfide for that purpofe; it differs from the hanging guard only in raifing the hand fomewhat higher, bringing the point nearer to yourfelf, and not fuffering it to fink below the height of your head. In this pofition the fort of your blade, which is to receive the blow, will be at leaft 3 or 4 inches above your head. The ward-iron of the hilt muft be turned well up to protect the knuckles. It will be proper to flip the right foot back to the left heel at the fame inftant.

Some perfons, inftead of keeping the fword advanced before them, raife the hand till the blade croffes above the head in an horizontal direction from right to left.

This

St. George's Guarde

Pub. as the act directs by I.Egerton Military Library Whitehall.

This latter pofition however is feldom ufed, and can hardly ever be neceffary, except to protect the head from a blow made by an antagonift behind, (for which purpofe it is adopted in the cavalry exercife) or to withdraw your weapon from one in front, who endeavours to feize it, and is un-armed himfelf.

Againft a blow made by a perfon in front, how-ever near, the firft defcribed pofition will be found preferable, raifing your fword-hand and point, ac-cording to circumftances.

It muft be obferved that the St. George's guard is not intended to lie under, but only to ftop a blow at the head, when your antagonift ftrikes fo much to the left of your pofition, that the hang-ing guard is not fufficiently fecure. The beft way in general of changing from the St. George (un-lefs when you immediately return a cut from it) is to adopt the hanging guard, taking care to direct your point towards the ribs of your antagonift,

E 2 and

and to keep your body well in a line. From
this pofition, there is lefs danger in taking another
than if you change directly from the **St.** George
to the **infide** or outfide guard.

SPADROON GUARD*

IS formed by dropping the point to the right
from the outfide guard, till it comes under the
adverfary's blade, turning your edge upwards at
the fame time, and raifing the wrift. It is fometimes ufed to prevent your antagonift difengaging
from the outfide guard under your wrift, and
planting a thruft below your guard, by following
his blade round, and coinciding with the motion
he gives to his weapon carrying it out of the line
to the left. But this in general is better oppofed

* Although this is denominated the *Spadroon* Guard, yet
it is not to be confidered as the chief pofture of defence with
that weapon. It is indeed the weakeft guard of any, and
fhould never be had recourfe to, but in fuch circumftances
as will not admit of immediately changing to another without danger of a time thruft or cut.

by

Spadroon Guard

Pub.^d as the act directs by I.Sewton Military Library Whitehall.

by fwiftly turning down to the *feconde* hanging guard; or by the *half circle* and *prime parades*, which will be defcribed when treating of the thrufts.

The pofition of the **fpadroon guard** being con-ftrained and weak, fhould **your** antagonift make a forcible beat on your blade, he will in all proba-bility difarm you. Therefore, inftead of receiving his blow in that pofition, flip it by withdrawing your weapon at the inftant he ftrikes at it, and re-turn cut II. at the outfide of his fword arm.

Caution however will be requifite, that you do **not** withdraw your fword inftead of parrying **a blow** aimed at yourfelf. The difference will de-pend on the diftance you are from your antagonift, and on his advancing or remaining ftationary. Al-ways quit this pofition as foon as poffible for the infide or outfide guard, in doing which fpring back **that your** antagonift may not throw in a cut by timing your change of pofition.

Having acquired the preceding guards, the next

articles

articles to be attended to are *bearing*, *battering*, the *feints* and *difarms*.

BEARING

I S generally practifed by lunging forward brifkly on the outfide guard, oppofing the fort of your blade to that of your antagonift, and from thence flipping your fort towards his feeble*, by which means you may prefs his fword out of the line; this (unlefs he takes to the hanging guard) leaves his head, neck and breaft expofed to your edge, and from this pofition a *cut over and within his guard* may be made, but muft be executed with celerity.

Bearing on an infide guard is fometimes practifed, but is not fo fafe, as the opponent may eafily drop his point, and fpringing back make cut III. at your arm.

---

* In attempting this, be careful not to flip your fword too far down, left your antagonift difengage and cut withinfide.

Upon

Upon the hanging guard *bearing* cannot be ufed to advantage, fince in bearing on an antagonift's blade to obtain an opening at the outfide of his pofition, you expofe your own head and infide, and by flipping from your bearing he will in all probability effect a cut.

BATTERING

IS ftriking on your antagonift's fword to obtain an opening, and requires the fame degree of caution as *bearing*, left your antagonift flip his blade from your ftroke, and make a cut on the contrary fide. It can feldom be attempted with fuccefs againft any but the outfide and fpadroon guards, when ufed to force an opening on the fide at which you batter; but fometimes by inducing an adverfary to refift that attack, you may difengage and cut on the contrary fide.

E 4

Of

Of FEINTS.

A FEINT is an offer at a cut or thruft without ftriking home. There are two forts, *fingle feints* and *double feints*. The fingle feint is made by difengaging from that fide on which you are oppofed by your adverfary's guard, and making a flight motion at the other, you then return to the firft and deliver the cut. For inftance, if engaged on the outfide guard, you will difengage over the point, and dropping your point on the infide of your adverfary's blade about fix inches, return to the outfide, and deliver cut II. at his arm, or VI. at his ribs. If you find him prepared to parry thofe cuts (II. and VI.) you will only make an offer as before, which conftitutes it a double feint, and deliver your cut at the head or infide of his pofition.

But as cutting at the infide againft an antagonift who is tolerably perfect in his guards, efpecially from feints, is attended with the danger of a counter-ftroke, I would recommend when you intend

tend a double feint to commence it by a difengage
from the infide.

The purpofe of feints being only to induce your
adverfary to guard a part at which you do not defign to ftrike, the feints, whether fingle or double,
may be directed at any other parts as well as thofe
mentioned. Great caution however is neceffary,
that in making your feints you do not uncover yourfelf fo much as to receive a time thruft or cut. The
feint fhould alfo be directed at a part from whence
you can quickly recover your weapon to effect the
cut you intend.

DISARMING.

THERE are various methods of difarming attempted, but the fafeft and moft likely to
fucceed is, after parrying an infide cut to change
quickly to the outfide, and lunging forward to bear
your adverfary's blade out of the line to the outfide,
then ftep with your left foot up to his right heel,
feize his fhell with your left hand, quit your bearing
on his blade, and prefent your point to his breaft.

Thofe

Those difarms which are to be effected by wrenching from an infide guard to a feconde hanging guard, or from an outfide guard to a half circle parade* will not often fucceed, except with very light fwords. With fuch, they mutt be commenced by turning the knuckles rather more up than ufual on thofe guards, and fwiftly reverfing them as you wrench the adverfary's blade down, directing your point rather in a diagonal line acrofs his body, than permitting it to form a circle. Thefe latter difarms are only applicable if the antagonift prefents his blade and arm nearly horizontal; and in that cafe, if they do not fucceed in wrenching the fword out of his hand, will prove ufeful to obtain an opening for a cut or thruft.

The method of avoiding them is by difengaging under your adverfary's hilt at the inftant he endeavours to crofs your blade. If this difengage be well timed, he may probably throw his own fword from his hand, by not meeting the refiftance he expected.

* Defcribed, page 75.

AP-

APPLICATION *of the* POINT.

THE weight of the broad fword will not permit the fame number of thrufts that may be
made with the fmall fword. All that can be fafely
introduced among the cuts of the former are four,
viz. *Carte*, *Tierce*, *Low Carte*, and *Seconde* which
is a low tierce: thefe fhould be thruft with the
hilt high enough to ward any blow your adverfary
may be likely to make, and to retard a difengage-
ment over your wrift at the inftant of lunging.

CARTE is thruft at the infide of the upper part
of the body, with the nails upward, and the edge
of the fword turned rather upward to the left,
and well oppofed towards your antagonift's weapon by keeping your pummel oppofite your left
temple at the time of lunging. *

* If when thrufting at the infide of your antagonift you
are apprehenfive of his cutting downwards, you muft turn
the wrift as in the fpadroon guard, that your ward-iron may
be upwards. In thrufting at the outfide, turn the wrift as
in the hanging guard.
Low

Low Carte is thruſt at the inſide of the lower half of your antagoniſt's body, with the ſame pre-caution of oppoſing your edge towards your adver-ſary's blade.

Tierce is thruſt at the upper part of your an-tagoniſt's body, over his arm, with your nails downward, the edge of your ſword turned to the right, and oppoſed towards his blade.

Seconde differs from tierce in being thruſt below the ſword arm.

In thruſting *Carte* and *Low Carte* be careful to form a good oppoſition toward your antagoniſt's weapon by carrying your wriſt to the left. In thruſting *Tierce* and *Seconde* the oppoſition to his blade muſt be formed by bearing your wriſt to the right. *

In

---

* Although in uſing the ſmall ſword, there are other thruſts which are made with the *back of the blade* oppoſed to the weapon of the antagoniſt, yet they cannot be executed with a broad ſword, without great hazard of receiving a cut

OR

In thrusting with the SABRE the safeft thrufts are thofe already recommended, fince the convex *edge* of the fabre, when oppofed to your antagonift's blade, affords protection from a counter cut or thruft. Yet the advantage that may fometimes be attained by the curve of the fabre enabling you to deceive your adverfary's guard deferves confidera-tion. For inftance—

Engage on an outfide guard, your edge op-pofed to mine : thruft at me, *turning your nails up-ward* as you lunge, this forms the thruft called *Carte over the Arm*, and brings the hollow back of your fabre againft my weapon, and thereby enables you to direct the point 6 or 8 inches more toward my left than you otherwife could, and to effect either a thruft, or a fawing cut at my face or neck.

on the arm at the time of lunging ; fince if your antagonift fprings back, his body will be out of the reach of your thruft, and your arm become expofed to his edge. This is not the cafe with the fmall fword, which being much lighter, the thruft and recovery to guard are executed with more celerity, and when oppofing another fmall fword with-out danger from the edge of your antagonift.

Obferve

Obferve, that as you deliver this thruft, your oppofition to my blade muft be formed by carrying
your wrift to the right of the line of defence.

If I parry this thruft, of carte over the arm,
by an outfide guard; the inftant your point paffes
the outfide of my pofition, I may cut II. at the
outfide of your fword arm; this you muft parry
by an outfide guard, or a *feconde* hanging guard:
or if I drop my point over your blade, and cut
at your cheek, you muft parry by a *prime* hanging
guard.

Some after parrying carte over the arm by an
outfide guard, whirl the blade round with a half
circle parade, and return low carte: this may be
eafily effected againft a perfon who is flow in recovering from his lunge.

Advantages fimilar to that in thrufting carte
over the arm may be obtained with a fabre by reverfing the wrift on the other thrufts: thefe may
be better underftood by taking the fabre in your
hand, and obferving the effect produced on the direction

rection of the point by turning your nails up and down, than by the moft accurate defcription. However, do not be too partial to this mode of obtaining an opening, but recollect, that in making a thruft on this principle, the ward-iron of your hilt will not be on the fide where you want the protection, and that if your thruft be parried, the pofition of your arm expofes you to the edge of your antagonift as you recover.

As thrufting is not the principal object of the broad fword, I fhall not trouble the reader farther on this head than to recommend his acquiring by practice a facility of making the before men-tioned in good pofition, directing the point with accuracy, and recovering to his guard with expedi-tion; for which purpofe it will be neceffary to practife at a target with the fword, fometimes thrufting only, at others cutting half way, and finifhing with a thruft : for inftance,

Cut I. half way, then turn up the nails and thruft carte, or low carte.

Cut

Cut II. about one third of the line, then turn down the nails and thrust tierce, or seconde.

Cut III. part of the line and thrust carte or low carte.

Cut IV. half way and thrust seconde.

By this practice the learner may not only attain accuracy in directing his point, but also a celerity in returning either a cut or thrust after having parried. He should frequently place himself out of reach of the target, that he may learn to recover from a thrust when parried; otherwise if he accustoms himself to find a support from his point always hitting the target, he will not acquire a proper method of recovering to guard.

Of

Of parrying Thrusts made above the Wrist.

THESE thrusts may be parried by an inside
or outside guard, striking your fort with an
abrupt beat on your adverfary's feeble, and retaining your point in the line of defence, prefented
to his face. In doing this, it will be proper to
fink your hilt rather lower than when oppofing
a cut, and to keep the arm fomewhat more flexible.

Of parrying Thrusts made below the Wrist.

THE most ufual method of parrying thrusts
made below the wrist, with a broad fword,
is to beat the opponent's blade to the outfide, by
dropping the point to a *feconde* hanging guard,
whether thofe thrusts be made by difengaging
from an outfide or infide guard.

In performing this parade, obferve to retain a
fufficient command of your fword to be able to

F   change

change quickly to a *prime* hanging guard by carrying your wrift to the left, if neceffary :. otherwife
your antagonift may deceive you by a feint, and
deliver his thruft at the infide.

This mode of parrying, firft with a *feconde*, and
then changing to a *prime* hanging guard if your
antagonift difengage to attack the infide of your
pofition, feems peculiarly adapted to the broad
fword, as the fituation of the hand at the fame
time affords great fecurity from a cut as well as a
thruft.

In fome circumftances, efpecially in an attack at
night, your fafety muft depend greatly on not
lofing the feel of your antagonift's blade ; you
fhould therefore learn to parry the lower thrufts
by following your antagonift's weapon with your
own blade,—with a *feconde* parade if he difengages
from an infide guard ; and with a *prime* or a *half
circle* parade, if he difengages from an outfide
guard.

Of following your Antagonist's Blade from the inside to parry with a SECONDE.

AS your antagonist drops his point from the inside guard, to thrust below your wrist, you
must follow his blade by taking the *seconde* hanging guard. Having parried his thrust, you may
turn up your nails and return cut V. under his
blade, or you may return a thrust in feconde.

If he completes the circle with his point by continuing the motion till he brings it over your hilt
to thrust at the infide, you must parry by changing
from the *feconde* to the *prime* hanging guard.

———

Of following your Antagonist's Sword with the PRIME PARADE.

AT the instant the antagonist sinks his point
from your outfide guard in order to thrust
under your wrist, drop your point over his blade,

and

and ftriking the back of your blade on his weapon, draw your hand to within a foot of your fore-head, in a line with your left temple, fo as to bring his thruft clear of the infide of your pofi-tion. To effect this you muft bend your elbow; then having brought his blade paft your body, ftraighten your arm to a hanging guard, turning the back of your hand oppofite your forehead. This fhould be practifed till you can perform it with readinefs as one motion.

The prime thruft may be frequently delivered with fafety after forming this parade. It differs from the thruft in feconde in being directed at the infide ihftead of at the outfide, and the oppofition to your antagonift's blade being formed by bear-ing your wrift to the left of the line of defence inftead of the right.

If you intend to return a thruft after having parried by the prime, it will be fafeft either to op-pofe your antagonift's blade with your left hand as you thruft; or to ftep out of the line to the

right

Prime Parade

Pub.^d as the act directs by T.Egerton Military Library Whitehall.

Half Circle Parade.

Pub.ᵈ as the act directs by I. Egerton Military Library Whitehall.

right as you parry, which gives you an opportunity of thrusting at the inside of your antagonist.

If your antagonist should only make a half thrust and disengage to the outside, you must oppose any cut or thrust he may there attempt, by carrying your hand to the right as in the *seconde* hanging guard.

HALF CIRCLE PARADE.

THIS is made by dropping your point over your adversary's blade as he quits your outside guard to thrust under your hilt, and striking with the *edge* of your sword against his blade, to beat his thrust past the inside. In performing this, the arm must be extended and inclined to the left till the wrist becomes opposite the left temple, the back of the hand downwards, and the point directed towards your antagonist's hip. When by this parade you have beat his blade out of the line to the left, you may turn the nails down and cut VI. in return beneath his blade as he recovers, springing back as you cut.

F 3

If

If in performing the half circle parade, you miss the feel of your adverfary's blade, by his raifing his point over your hilt to thruft at your outfide, you muft inftantly carry your hand about fix inches to the right or outfide of your line of defence, the infide of the wrift ftill upwards, and oppofe his thruft with the back of your blade; then whirl your point up in a circular direction outwards, and thus bring it round to the *feconde* hanging guard, without finking your wrift as you turn it.

Obferve to keep the gripe encircled with your forefinger and thumb, or you will be liable to lofe your fword. Hold your head well back and incline your body on the left hip. This parade may be practifed alone with your fword, till you can perform it rapidly and without any paufe.

If in whirling your blade up, you beat your antagonift's weapon out of the line; then, inftead of dropping your point to form a *feconde*, make cut II. at his head or arm.

One material objection to ufing the half circle parade againft a perfon armed with a cut and
thruft

thruft fword arifes from the opportunity it may afford him of bringing you to that parade by a feint, in order to effect a cut at your arm: if he lifts his point for that purpofe, you muft fpring off with your edge and ward-iron upwards, as in the fpadroon guard, p. 60, and inftantly change to an infide or outfide guard.

ROUND PARADES.

THESE cannot be well performed with a very heavy fword, yet will prove ufeful to a perfon armed with a fpadroon or light cut and thruft fword.

Engage on an infide guard:—Your antagonift difengages to thruft tierce or carte over the arm; follow his blade by defcribing a fmall circle with your point, keeping your wrift on the line of the infide guard: this will bring his blade to the pofition from which he difengaged.—Obferve this circle is began by finking your point from *left to right.*

On an outfide guard:—Your opponent difengages to thruft carte; follow his blade with a fmall circle began by dropping your point from the *right to the left*, keeping your wrift on the outfide guard : this alfo brings his blade up to the pofition from which he difengaged.

N. B. The motion of your wrift and the circle defcribed by your point muft not be greater than may be fufficient to enable you to preferve or regain the feel of your antagonift's weapon : for which reafon, when you intend to ufe thefe parades againft a thruft, you muft engage with your point directed towards the upper part of your antagonift's breaft.

CIRCLE PARADE.

THIS is formed by defcribing a circle of about three feet diameter with your point, keeping your wrift the height of your fhoulder, on the line of either an infide or outfide guard, your weight refting on the left leg, and holding your head back. This parade is extremely ferviceable for regaining the feel of an adverfary's blade, efpecially when engaged in the dark, and will be found ufeful againft a perfon who may endeavour to embarrafs you by a multiplicity of feints.

It may now be neceffary to notice fuch cuts as deviating from the principles of the fyftem become exceptions to every general rule, and therefore demand particular attention.

Of this defcription are thofe cuts in which we abandon *that general principle of fecurity of cutting towards an antagonift's blade in order to prevent a counter ftroke or time thruft.* Under this head may be claffed the three following cuts, in which fecurity is to be attained by firft throwing an adverfary's blade out of the line.

———————

Cut V. *under the Sword.*

IF on the infide guard your antagonift lowers his point and prefents his arm and blade in a line nearly horizontal, fo that you can crofs about 8 inches of his feeble with your fort, drop your blade fmartly acrofs his, and wrench his fword to the outfide under your blade, then turn your wrift and cut V. beneath his blade and recover to an outfide guard.

(In

(In order to be able to perform this cut with
safety and effect, it will be neceſſary frequently to
practiſe alone with a ſword, dropping the point
from an inſide guard to a *ſeconde* hanging guard,
then turning up the nails cut V. and recover to an
outſide guard.)

If your antagoniſt be aware of your deſign, he
will probably withdraw his blade or diſengage under your wriſt : in which caſe you muſt ſpring
back on a hanging guard the inſtant you loſe the
feel of it, preſenting your point at his ribs, or
ſeek his ſword by the circle parade.

The parade to this cut is formed by raiſing the
point and dropping your hilt low to an inſide guard,
upon feeling your point borne out of the line, in
which caſe the perſon who attempts the cut muſt
alſo recover to an inſide guard.

Cut

Cut VI. *under the Sword.*

WHEN you are on the outfide guard and your antagonift prefents his point low, as before defcribed, drop your blade fmartly acrofs his as if to make cut III. wrench his blade to the left, and then quitting it, turn the wrift and cut VI. under his fword acrofs the body, recovering to the infide guard or to a hanging guard.

Unlefs this be well executed it is fomewhat dan_ gerous, efpecially if your antagonift fufpect your defign and withdraw his blade or difengage; fhould he do that, you may fpring back on the fpadroon guard the inftant you lofe the feel of it; or regain his fword by the circle parade.

This, as well as the preceding cut, will require practifing alone with a fword, firft dropping the point as in the half circle parade, and then making cut VI. and recovering to an infide or a hanging guard.

The

The parade to cut VI. thus given beneath the fword, muft be made by raifing your point and dropping the hilt low to an outfide guard, on the inftant you are borne out of the line. When the cut is thus ftopped, the perfon who attempts it muft alfo take an outfide guard.

Although it is not to be fuppofed that in an attack at firft a fkilful antagonift will be very likely to prefent his blade and arm in the horizontal direction defcribed in the two preceding leffons; neverthelefs the method here recommended will prove ufeful, as a practice for improvement, in order to attain a celerity in returning a cut after having parried a thruft either by the *half circle* parade or *feconde* hanging guard.

Cut

Cut V. over and within the Sword.

IF at any time on the outfide guard your antagonift holds his wrift too low, bear his blade
a little out of the line, and turning the back of
your blade to the back of his, cut V. above his
fword acrofs the neck, retreating as you cut.*

This muft be parried by raifing the hand quickly
to a prime hanging guard.

Your antagonift having parried your cut by the
hanging guard, your feeble will become oppofed
to his fort : unlefs you withdraw it very quickly,
he may whirl your blade outwards, and make
cut V. at your face, or thruft carte over the arm :
if he attempts either, parry by the hanging guard,
and return a thruft in feconde as he recovers.

* A fimilar cut to this may fometimes be effeéted againft
an infide guard, but as that is the ftrongeft guard which can
be held, will not often fucceed.

The

The CUT *at the advanced* LEG *or* THIGH.

THIS cut can feldom be made without confiderable danger to the perfon who attempts it againft a fwordfman, as it muft be always attended with an inclination of the body, and the head being thus brought forward, becomes expofed, even when the leg or thigh at which the ftroke is directed, is removed out of diftance.

It fhould never be attempted without previoufly diverting your antagonift's blade by a feint at the upper part of his pofition, and in that cafe may afford variety of play to gentlemen in friendly affaults for mutual diverfion, and will fo far be neceffary in order to attain the parade againft it; but will always be extremely hazardous with the fword in real conteft, unlefs your antagonift advances his right foot by ftanding much too wide upon guard. Otherwife, in ftriking at his leg, your head and fword arm muft become expofed even to a perfon wholly ignorant of the

fcience,

science, and his attention not being occupied by endeavouring to parry, his blow at the head would probably prove fatal, even though he received a cut on the leg at the same instant.

I must however observe that in attempting it a considerable degree of safety may be attained by raising the hand, as in the hanging guard, when cutting at the outside of the leg, and sinking the body behind the protection of the hilt; and, when cutting at the inside turning the wrist in the position of the spadroon guard. But to effect this requires a very great degree of practice and agility.

Having mentioned the dangers to which this attempt is liable, I shall now describe the method of executing it in the safest manner according to the opinion of an able writer on this science, without fear of its being adopted rashly in a real contest.

" The first method is to parry an inside cut, and instead of returning an outside, step a little forwarder, sinking your body at the same time you
transfer

transfer your weight from the left to the right leg, bring the point underneath your adverſary's ſword, and cutting ſwiftly at the calf of his leg, ſpring back as from a longe under cover of a St. George or hanging guard. This throw ſhould never be uſed againſt a maſter of *timing*, for if he ſlip his right leg inſtead of parrying, he may cut you either on the head or arm.

"The ſecond way of going down to the leg is by much the ſafeſt of the two, and is done by ſinking the body very low at half ſword under a St. George's guard, make a feint to the leg, recover to a St. George, feint to the leg again, then ſtopping fully with a St. George go ſwiftly down to the leg, and ſpring off as before."

A very trifling reflection on the openings afforded to your adverſary's point as well as his edge, by this manœuvre, which the author ſtiles the *ſafeſt*, will certainly prevent its being too haſtily adopted.

Parade

Parade against the Cuts at the Leg or Thigh.

If you are upon the inside or outside guard. At the
inftant your antagonift drops his wrift to make the
cut, flip the right foot back to the left heel, and meet
the infide of his fword arm with cut III, if he cuts
at the infide of your leg or thigh. Make cut IV,
if he ftrikes at the outfide.

Should you have any reafon to fufpect the offer at
your leg to be only a feint, prefent your point oppofite to the face of your antagonift, drawing in
the fword arm a little on either an infide or outfide
guard, (according to which fide your adverfary
may threaten) and retiring the leg. His intention
may generally be difcovered by his inclining the
head and body forwards if he means to cut; and
retaining them when only making a feint.

Some perfons, when they fufpect the offer at the
leg to be only a feint, prefent the point to the antagonift's face, and *extend* the fword arm, in order

to prevent his advancing too clofe to be avoided by flipping the leg. This method muft, however, be ufed with caution againft a fwordfman; for when you thus prefent your blade and arm horizontal, if your antagonift fhould ftrike his fort fmartly againft your feeble, he may beat your blade upwards and deliver a low thruft.

If you are upon the hanging guard, and your antagonift has advanced too near to be avoided by flipping the leg, drop your point fo as to meet his edge with yours, retiring the leg in the manner above directed, and as foon as you have parried, make Cut I. or II.

REMARKS

REMARKS on the SPADROON.

THE spadroon being much lighter than the broad sword, and made both to cut and thrust, is therefore a weapon well adapted to those gentlemen who are masters both of the small and broad sword, and unite according to circumstances the defensive and offensive movements of the two. In thrusting, the spadroon has an advantage over the broad sword, on account of the celerity with which that fatal movement may be executed, but in cutting it is much weaker in its effect.

The chief defensive position of the spadroon among the French, resembles the *seconde* hanging guard, except that the blade is held more horizontal, the point is directed at the antagonist's body about two inches below the arm-pit, and the wrist held on a level with the shoulder, instead of raising it high enough to view your adversary under the shell.

From

From this guard, by dropping the point to the inside or outside of your position, as in the *prime* or *seconde* hanging guard, you may parry any cut or thrust made below the neck. Cuts at the head are parried by the *St. George,* those made at the cheek and neck by raising the hilt to a *prime* or *seconde* hanging guard, as with the broad sword.

Much practice will be necessary to enable you to hold the sword in the position above described, without constraint or wavering, and to attain the *firmness* requisite for parrying, and a sufficient degree of *celerity* in striking or thrusting.

The left hand should be placed with the palm flat on the left hip bone, in order to preserve the balance. The center of gravity must be thrown on the left leg, and the feet placed as directed for the broad sword.

Although the above guard in *seconde* is that on which the most eminent French masters place the chief dependence, and in which they princi-

pally

pally inftruct their fcholars; yet the guards mentioned in the preceding work for the broad fword,
will be found equally ufeful, efpecially to thofe
who cannot retain their arm a fufficient length of
time in that pofture.

In adopting the infide and outfide guards to
parry a thruft, remember to fink the hand rather
lower than when oppofing a cut at the arm, and
keep your point prefented to your adverfary's face.

The *cuts* with the fpadroon are made on a principle fimilar to thofe of the broad fword, except
in the following inftances. The weapon being
lighter and the blade held more horizontal, the
difengaging may be effected with a fmaller circle
defcribed by the point, and the attack made more
rapidly.

The mode of recovering from cuts I. and II.
when you chance to mifs the object at which your
cut is directed may be rather more in front than
with the broad fword or fabre, inftead of the blade

fwinging

swinging so much round to the outside or inside of
your position, as is neceffary with those weapons.
To facilitate this method of recovering, cuts I.
and II. with the fpadroon may be made with a circular direction; whereas the weight of the fabre
renders it difficult to apply the edge unlefs the cut
be made in a more direct line.

One cut *withinfide the arm* feems indeed peculiar
to the fpadroon, fince few have fufficient ftrength
in the arm to effect it with the broad fword. It
is thus performed; your antagonift being on a feconde hanging guard, feint a thruft in feconde,
and if he attempts to parry it with his feeble, turn
your nails up without difengaging, and raifing your
point cut at the infide of his fword arm. This
cut, if performed with fpirit, is generally fure to difable; and is rendered fafe, by your antagonift's
feeble being occupied in a vain attempt to bear
out your fort, which is brought againft his feeble
by your longeing forward as you raife your point.
If he finks his hand to parry with his fort, fpring
off

off with a cut at the upper part of his arm, on the outfide.

The moſt eligible thruſts to be made with the ſpadroon are thoſe already recommended, p. 67, for the broad ſword.—Thoſe who wiſh to become perfeɛt maſters of the ſpadroon ſhould however be acquainted alſo with the ſyſtem of the ſmall ſword, on which there are already ſo many treatiſes publiſhed, that it is unneceſſary to ſwell this work with further remarks on the ſubjeɛt.——That publiſhed by Mr. Angelo, intitled the School of Fencing, is indeed ſo clear and comprehenſive, that it cannot be too much recommended to thoſe who are deſirous of attaining a juſt idea of that art, and yet may not be able to attend regularly to leſſons from a fencing maſter.

In retiring from a ſuperior force, the mode taught by the French of flouriſhing the weapon is ſtiled *a la debandade*, and conſiſts in brandiſhing it in front of your poſition from right to left, turning the wriſt up and down ſo as to lead with a

true

true edge, the point defcribing the figure ∞, the wrift held level with the fhoulder. By this method an antagonift may be prevented advancing too faft upon you, as he muft firft ftop the motion of your blade before he can fafely attack, and the next ftep you retreat again fets your weapon at liberty.

The practifing this figure alone with a fword, will tend much to fupple the wrift, and to give you a proper command of your weapon. It fhould be performed fometimes in the manner of cut I and II combined; at others as cut III and IV, only in a direction more horizontal.

APPENDIX

APPENDIX.

Oppofing the Small Sword.

IN contending with a broad fword againft a fmall
fword, your firft objeét fhould be to difable your
antagonift's fword arm if poffible, keeping your
body well back, and fpringing off at the inftant he
longes, far enough to remove your body from his
thruft, cut at his arm. Be cautious not to make
wide motions or to ftrike with too much exertion ;
and recover to your guard with your point well oppofed to his face.

When you parry a thruft by the infide or outfide guard, remember to fink the hilt lower than
when oppofing a cut.

If your antagonift difengages from an infide
guard,

guard, and thrufts below your wrift, follow his blade by dropping your point to the feconde hanging guard, and having parried his thruft to the outfide of your pofition, turn your wrift, and before he recovers from his longe cut V. beneath his blade. If from the outfide guard he lowers his point to thruft beneath the hilt, parry with the half circle or prime parade, and cut VI. under his blade.

Should your antagonift be fo near when on the above longe as not to allow fufficient fweep to give cuts V. and VI. with force; in that cafe, inftead of ftriking, draw your fword edge fwiftly acrofs his body, retreating or traverfing at the inftant.

Obferve that after parrying a thruft made at you with a fmall fword, your chief advantage lies in returning a cut without longeing forward, becaufe your antagonift will always endeavour to recover from his longe with his point directed towards your body. This renders it neceffary to confine your attack particularly to his fword arm, except

when

when you may be able to beat his fword firft out of the line; otherwife if you longe eagerly to effect a cut at his head or body, you will rufh on his point. If you have an opportunity of ftriking on the back of his blade, as he recovers from a longe, you may probably difarm him.

Oppofing the Spadroon.

To oppofe this weapon, you muft be mafter of the parades againft the thrufts (defcribed p. 73 to 80,) fince thrufting is a principal object with the fpadroon. Should your antagonift's weapon be much fhorter than your own, be always ready to fpring off from an attempt to inclofe, otherwife he will get within your point, and the length of your fword will prove a material difadvantage.

Many perfons ufe the fpadroon in a manner very fimilar to that already defcribed for the broad fword, againft thofe the guards and cautions before mentioned will be fufficient. I fhall there-

fore

fore only obferve that in contending with fuch as
depend on the guard in *feconde*, it will be beft to
engage them with the hand in the pofition of the
infide guard, the fort of your blade croffing above
your antagonift's feeble, and your point about
eight inches to the right of your line of defence,
threatening the infide of his pofition.* At the fame
time fink on your knees, keeping your body well
poifed, and your left hand on your hip, but do not
reft too much weight on your right foot, left you
fhould be unable to withdraw it or to fpring off
when neceffary.

If your antagonift endeavours to thruft under
your hilt, parry by finking your hand on an outfide guard. If he difengages under your hilt,
your hand is already on an infide guard, and you
have only to raife your point to his right eye. If

* Your point would otherwife be oppofed to your adverfary's hilt, and both weapons in parallel lines, by which you
would lofe your principle of defence, which muft always depend in a great meafure on the crofs your weapon forms to
that of your antagonift.

he

he difengages over your point, he muft expofe the infide of his pofition and fword arm.

In attacking the fpadroon when held in *feconde*, the eafieft cut to effect will be on the outfide of the fword arm, firft making a light feint at the head or infide of the face, but be careful not to make wide motions.

Another cut may be effected by attacking the feeble of his blade brifkly with your fort, and beating it *downwards to the outfide of his pofition,* then turn your wrift and cut VI. at his ribs, recovering to an infide guard.

The mode of commencing with a cut and finifhing with a thruft (p. 71, 72.) will be found ufeful againft this guard of the fpadroon. If your antagonift holds his thumb on the back of the gripe, when on this guard of feconde, you may difarm him by making cut III. at the feeble of his blade. In performing this keep out of diftance of a longe.

It

It will not be prudent to attempt beating the fpadroon to the outfide of your pofition, becaufe your antagonift can eafily flip from that beat and thruft at your infide; neither would I recommend the broad fword hanging guard to be oppofed to the fpadroon, except merely to ftop a cut; for the fpadroon is fo much lighter and fwifter in its motions, that by repeated feints your arm will tire, and your antagonift foon gain an advantage, from your not being able to anfwer his motions with fufficient celerity.*

* The *feconde* hanging guard, with a long heavy fword, will not afford you fo much real protection againft the point of a determined adverfary, as it may, at firft view of the pofition, be thought to do. This difadvantage arifes from the eafe with which he may attack your feeble with his fort and beat it out of the line of defence, by which he gains an opening to thruft carte, or low carte. To avoid this attack, you may raife your point with a circular motion over his blade at the inftant he ftrikes at your feeble; and having thus flipped from his ftroke, return a thruft in feconde, or a cut at his outfide; fhould your blade be too heavy to effect this, fpring off. If you are aware of his intention time enough, the beft method of refifting his attack will be to drop your point and incline your hand towards the *prime* hanging guard, meeting his blow with your edge. In performing this do not make your motion too wide, nor bend your arm unneceffarily, left your antagonift effect a cut at the outfide of your arm.

Oppofing

Opposing the Musquet and Bayonet.

It will be in general best to parry the bayonet to the outside by dropping your blade across the barrel of the musket as in a hanging guard, the back of your fort close behind the elbow of the bayonet. The purchase thus obtained will assist your stepping forward with the left foot to seize the barrel with the left hand, which being once effected, places your adversary's life in your power.

In this method it is to be observed that although your parade may not have weight enough to beat the bayonet far out of the line of defence, yet by stepping about with your left foot, you change the line of defence, while your blade prevents your antagonist from withdrawing his weapon, or following your motion with his point.

Another method by which the thrust of a bayonet may be parried, is by opposing the fort

of

of the bayonet with that of your fword on an infide guard, and beating the bayonet towards the
left of the line of defence, feize it with your left
hand. But in performing this, unlefs you are very
quick, your adverfary may deceive you by difengaging under the hilt of your fword.

Engaging with Sticks.

As it may happen that a gentleman may be compelled to defend himfelf with a common walking
ftick, againft a ruffian who may prefume on his
fkill in cudgel playing, the following hints may
prove ufeful, in pointing out fuch deviations from
the general fyftem of broad fword as are requifite
to be known in that cafe.

In a conteft with fticks, if you parry with an infide or outfide guard, you muft endeavour to
meet your antagonift's blow with your fort, rather
more to the left or right of the line of defence, according to which fide you are protecting, than with
a fword. By thefe means the recoil of the fticks
will prevent the blow fliding down to your knuckles,
and

and in proportion as you can ſtop your antagoniſt's blow wide of the line of defence, you obtain a greater opening to return it.

The hanging guard is however the moſt uſual,
and often the ſafeſt, as it affords more protection
to the head and face, at which blows with a ſtick
are generally directed. The only difference in
holding this guard with a ſtick inſtead of a ſword
conſiſts in directing the point about ſix inches
towards the outſide of your antagoniſt's right hip,
inſtead of oppoſite his ſide; becauſe the point of a
ſtick, if held ſtationary like the point of a ſword,
will not prevent his advancing; but on the contrary may be ſeized with his left hand.

Among cudgel players the blows from this poſition are effected by a turn of the wriſt differing
from that uſed with the broad ſword, the *large*
knuckles of the hand (inſtead of the *middle* ones)
being directed towards the object at which the
blow is diſcharged, and turned downwards at the
inſtant of making it. If the opponent ſprings off
from a blow made in this manner, the general con-

H   ſequence

fequence to the affailant is a ftrain of the wrift, or
the lofs of his ftick. Another material difadvantage in this mode of ftriking is, that unlefs
they engage very clofe they cannot reach to hit
their antagonift.

When contending with a perfon who endeavours
to advance for this purpofe, receive his blows on
your hanging guard, and return a thruft beneath
his arm either at his face, right fide, or belly,
griping your ftick very firm that your thruft may
be of fufficient force; recover quickly to a hanging guard.

Cudgel players feldom pay much attention to
protecting the outfide of their right arm or ribs.
It will not however be fafe to ftrike at their outfide
except in returning a blow which you have juft parried. If you commence an attack at that part, you
will moft probably receive a cut in the face at the
fame inftant. The beft method therefore is to receive and return a few blows on the hanging guard,
and alternately intermix your play with cutting at

the

the wrift and elbow, and thrufting, thus keeping them at a greater diftance than they have been accuftomed to; and if you can by this mode of attack induce them to defend their ribs, feint at their outfide and throw at the head.

Very few cudgel players accuftom themfelves to longe at the time of ftriking, therefore if you can keep them at proper diftance, you will be out of their reach while they are within yours.

Should your antagonift fucceed in rufhing clofe up to you, notwithftanding all your endeavours to keep him at proper diftance, you may eafily difarm him at the inftant he clofes.

If he advances on a hanging guard, oppofe him with the fame guard; lower your body by fuddenly bending your knees, and pafs your left hand under your right wrift, feize his ftick, advance your left foot and knee behind his right, and dart the pummel of your ftick in his face, ftriking up his right foot at the fame inftant.

Or as your opponent advances, you may thruft

your

your left arm into the upper angle formed by the
crofs of your weapons, twine your arm round his,
by paffing your hand under his wrift and over his
arm, and bear it downwards. Ufe your pummel
and left foot as before.

If he advances on an outfide guard, lay hold of
his ftick with your left hand, and pull it downwards over your own, at the fame time dropping
your point and raifing your weapon forcibly to
the pofition of the feconde hanging guard.

There are other methods of difarming by advancing the left band and foot, but thefe are the
eafieft and moft readily executed, as they require
only a previous refleⅅion on the pofition, to enable
a perfon to adopt them whenever there may be
occafion.

F I N I S.

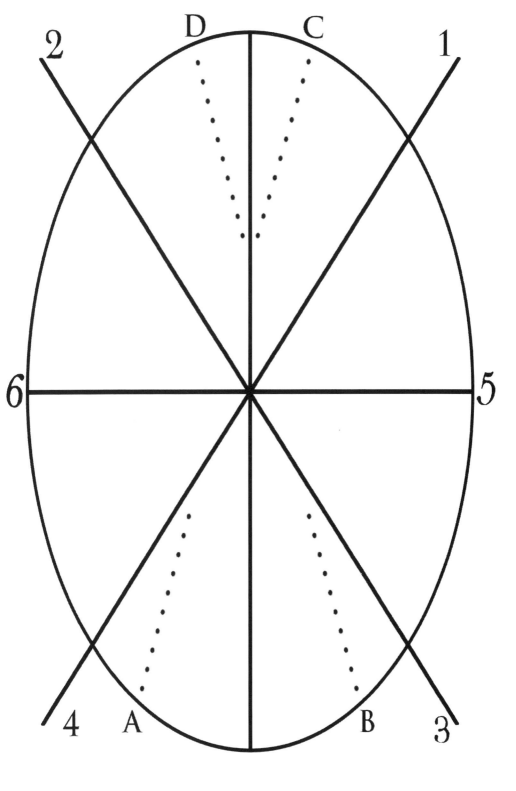

Inside Guard.

Editor's Note: This page is a reproduction of the image on page 50b of the original treatise. Since the method of binding for this facsimile meant that the spine interrupted the image and obscured the crossing of the swords, and required the caption to be moved, we wanted to show what the image looks like without such interruption. This page is provided for your convenience; the image did not appear for a second time at the end of the original book.

Outside Guards.

Editor's Note: This page is a reproduction of the image on page 52b of the original treatise. Since the method of binding for this facsimile meant that the spine interrupted the image and obscured the crossing of the swords, and required the caption to be moved, we wanted to show what the image looks like without such interruption. This page is provided for your convenience; the image did not appear for a second time at the end of the original book.